WOOF-WOOF HERE

GUAU-GUAU THERE

Ariadna Puchiu

Special thanks to talented Veronika Novskaya who drew the cute characters.

Text copyright ©2020 by Ariadna Puchiu

Parents and educators visit us on the web parenthink.org

Woof-Woof Here, Guau-Guau There First Edition

For Mihai my partner in fun, love & wild adventures and our awesome sons Sorin and Radu

The idea for this book started with a dog, Lucky, and three friends. Even though Lucky made the same barking sound, Alice, Joao and I - each from a different country - started a friendly argument: "Is it woof-woof?" or "Is it au-au?" or maybe "It is ham-ham".

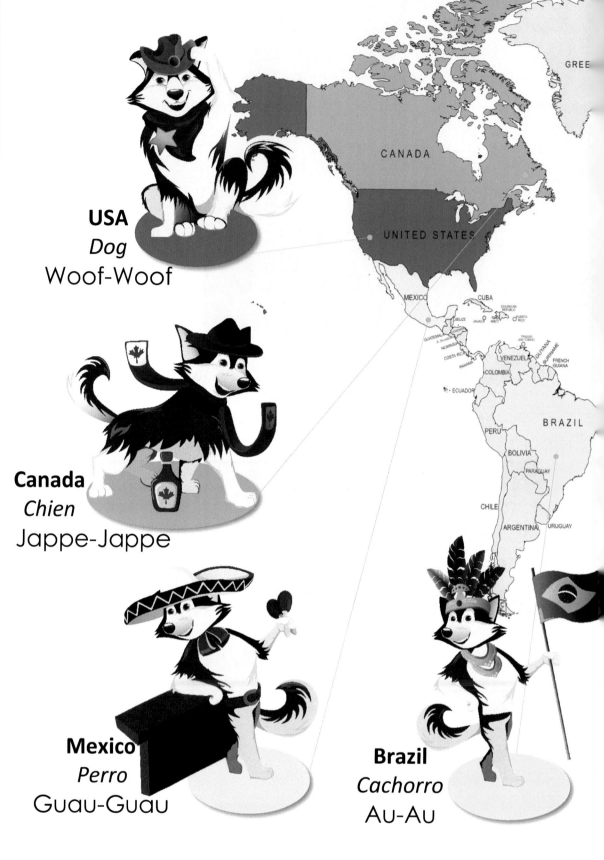

USA
Dog
Woof-Woof

Canada
Chien
Jappe-Jappe

Mexico
Perro
Guau-Guau

Brazil
Cachorro
Au-Au

🐕 A group of dogs is called a pack

🐕 A male dog is called a dog.

🐕 A female dog is called a dam.

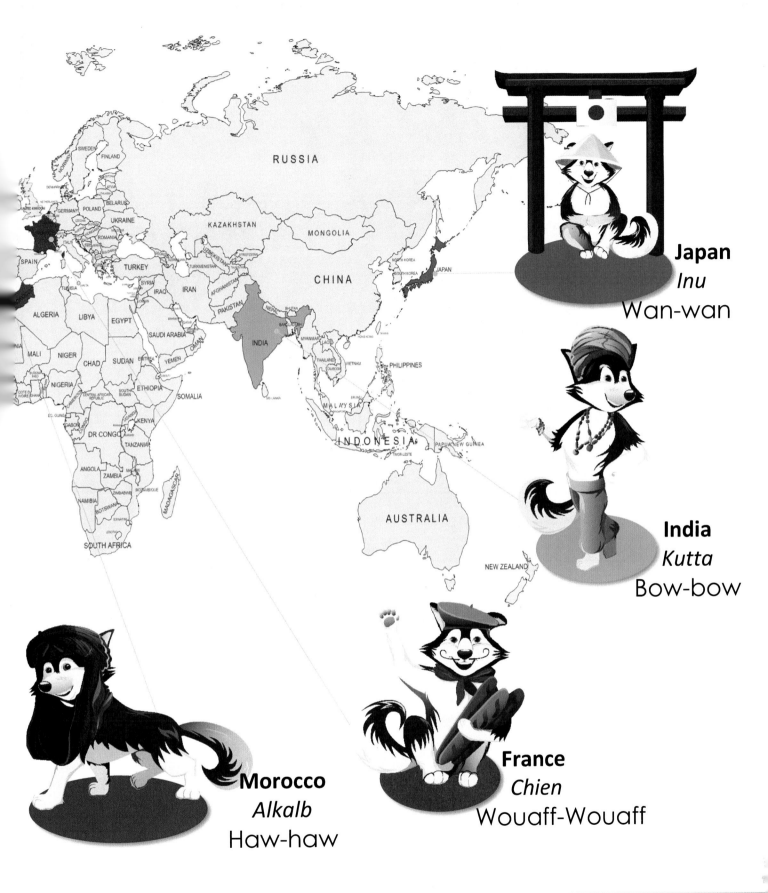

Japan
Inu
Wan-wan

India
Kutta
Bow-bow

Morocco
Alkalb
Haw-haw

France
Chien
Wouaff-Wouaff

A baby dog is called a Puppy

Fun fact: The Beatles song "A Day in the Life" has a frequency only dogs can hear. Watch your dog when you play the song!

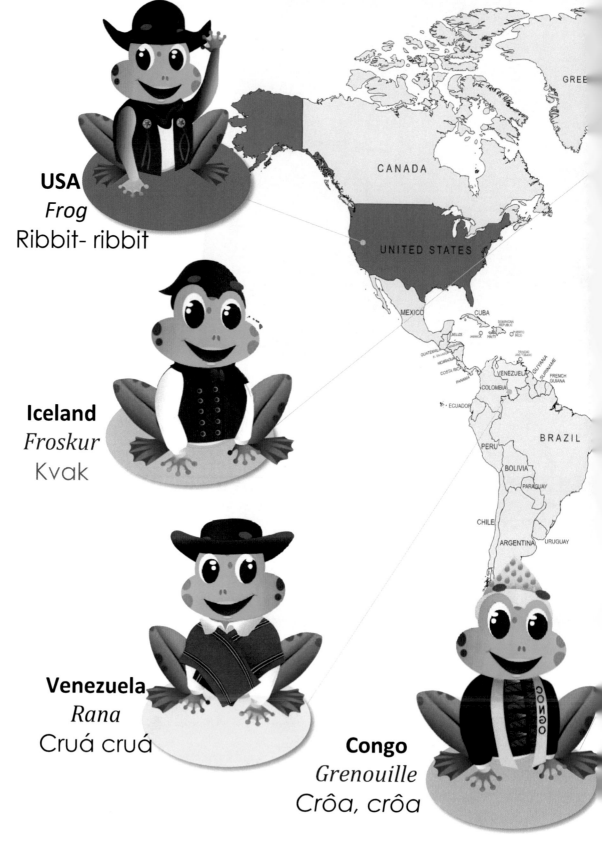

USA
Frog
Ribbit- ribbit

Iceland
Froskur
Kvak

Venezuela
Rana
Cruá cruá

Congo
Grenouille
Crôa, crôa

🐸 A group of frogs is called an army.

🐸 A male frog is called a male frog, or a toad.

🐸 A female frog is called a female frog, or a frog.

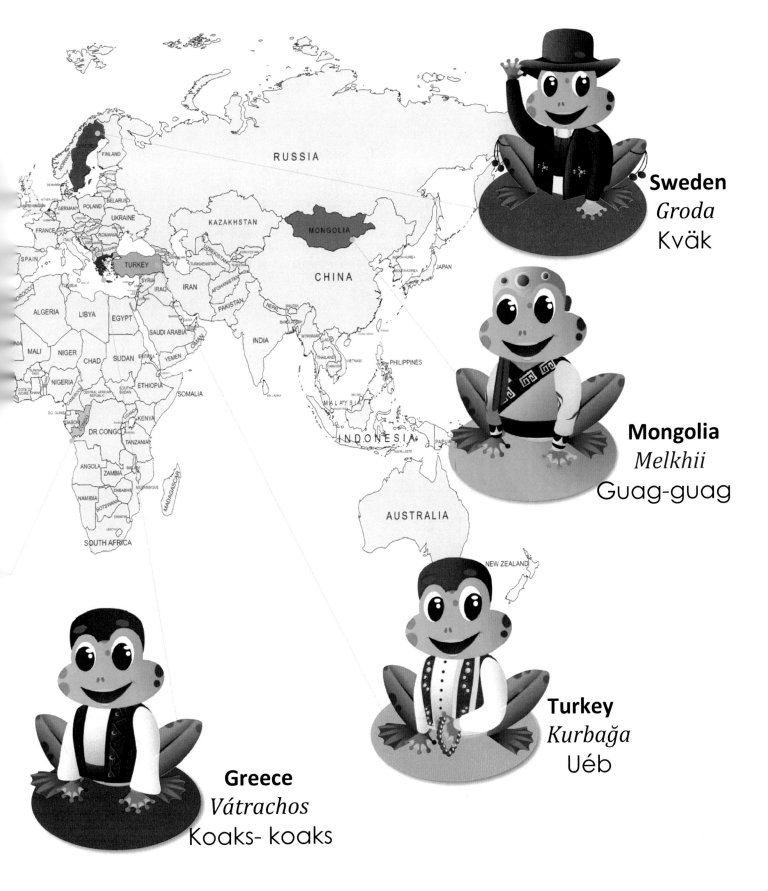

Sweden
Groda
Kväk

Mongolia
Melkhii
Guag-guag

Turkey
Kurbağa
Uéb

Greece
Vátrachos
Koaks- koaks

🐸 A baby frog is called a tadpole, or a froglet.
🐸 Fun fact: Launched by their long legs, many frogs can leap more than 20 times their body length.

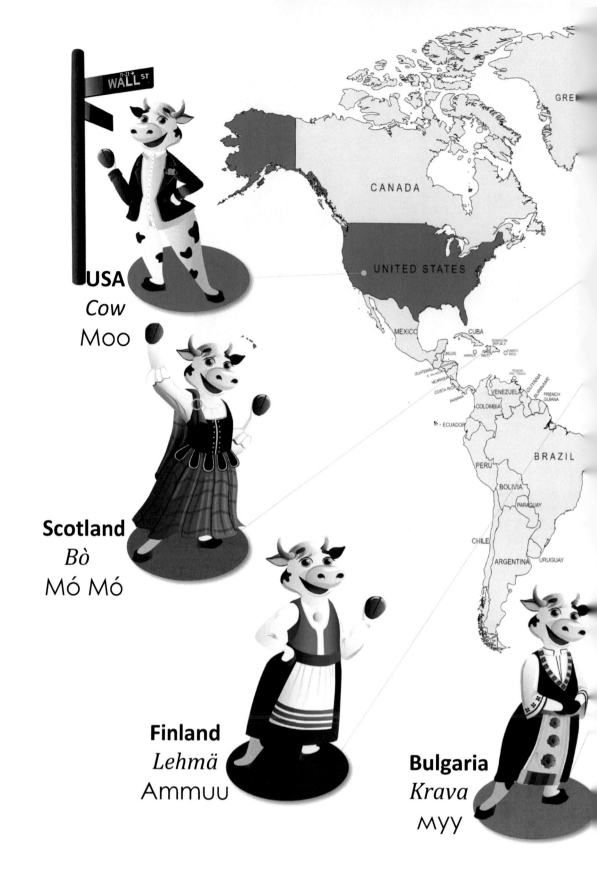

USA
Cow
Moo

Scotland
Bò
Mó Mó

Finland
Lehmä
Ammuu

Bulgaria
Krava
Myy

A group of cows is called a herd.

A male cow is called a bull.

A female cow is called a cow, or a heifer.

Korea
So
Eum-mae

Vietnam
Con bò cái
Um bò

Pakistan
Ga'ū
Hamma

Bangladesh
Gābhī
Hamba

A baby cows is called a calf.

Fun fact: Cows are very social and do not like to be alone.

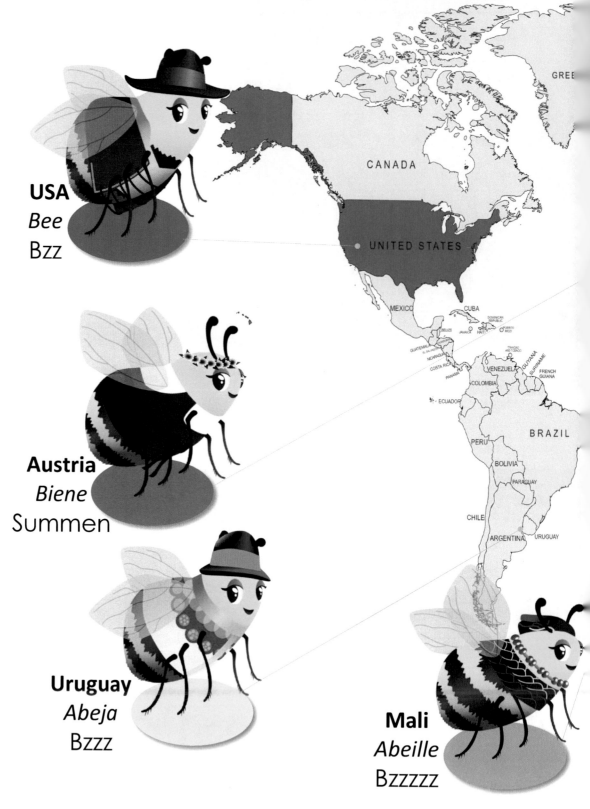

USA
Bee
Bzz

Austria
Biene
Summen

Uruguay
Abeja
Bzzz

Mali
Abeille
Bzzzzz

 A group of bees is called a colony, a nest, a swarm, or a bike.

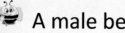 A male bee is called a drone.

 A female bee is called a worker bee or a queen bee.

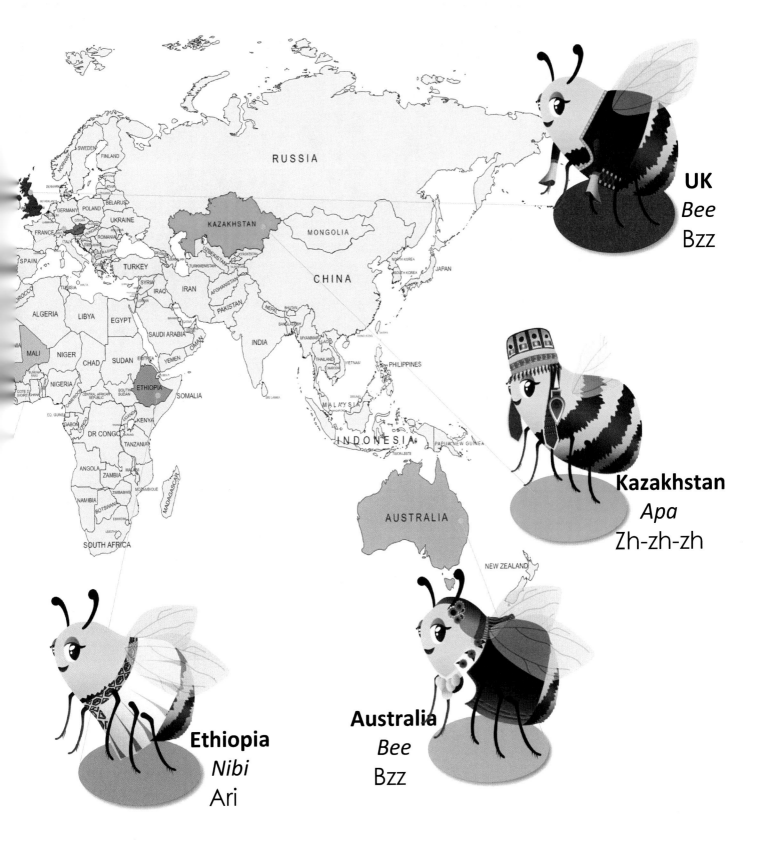

UK
Bee
Bzz

Kazakhstan
Apa
Zh-zh-zh

Ethiopia
Nibi
Ari

Australia
Bee
Bzz

 A baby bee is called a larva.

 Fun fact: Newborn bees ask for food by sticking out their tongues at passing worker bees.

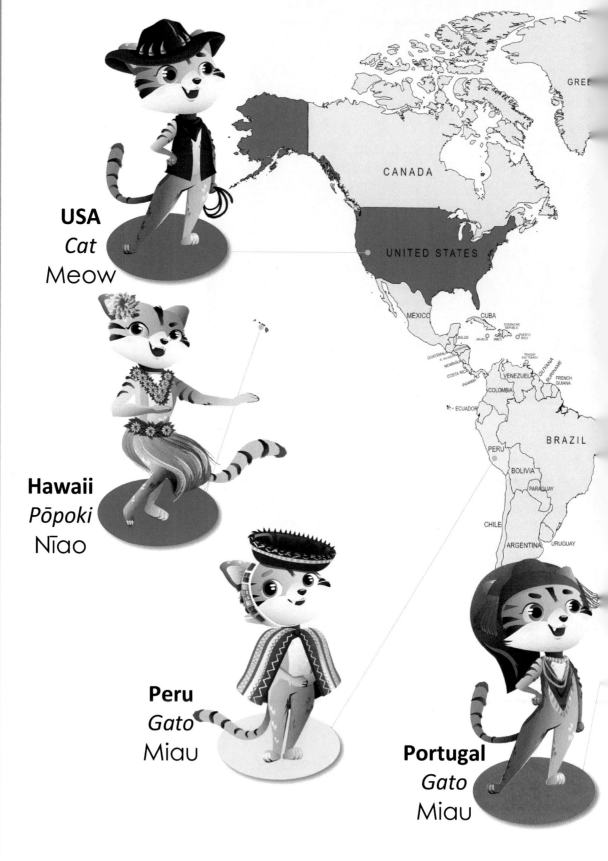

USA
Cat
Meow

Hawaii
Pōpoki
Nīao

Peru
Gato
Miau

Portugal
Gato
Miau

A group of cats is called a clowder.

A male cat is called a tom or tomcat.

A female cat is called a molly or a queen.

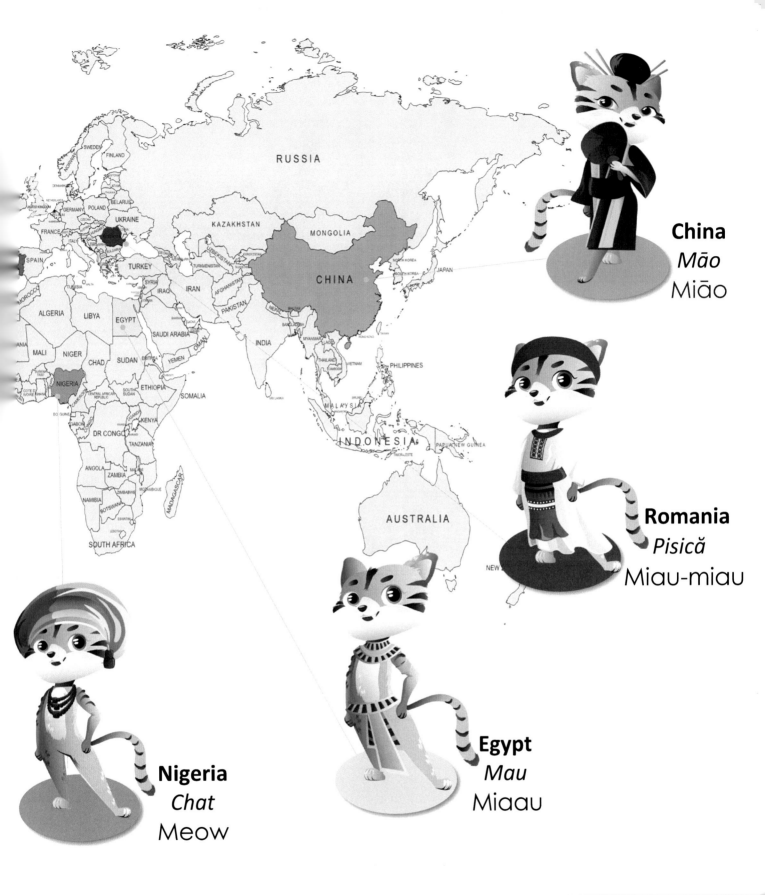

China
Māo
Miāo

Romania
Pisică
Miau-miau

Egypt
Mau
Miaau

Nigeria
Chat
Meow

A baby cat is called a kitten.

Fun fact: On October 18th 1963 Felicette, also known as 'Astrocat', was the first and only cat to go to space.

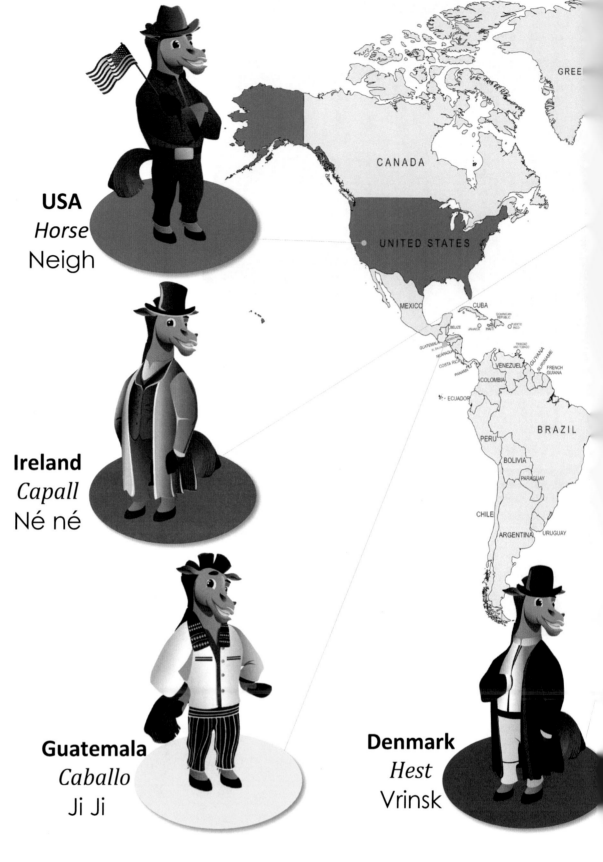

USA
Horse
Neigh

Ireland
Capall
Né né

Guatemala
Caballo
Ji Ji

Denmark
Hest
Vrinsk

 A group of horses is called a team or a harras.

A male horse is called a horse or a stallion.

A female horse is called a filly or a mare.

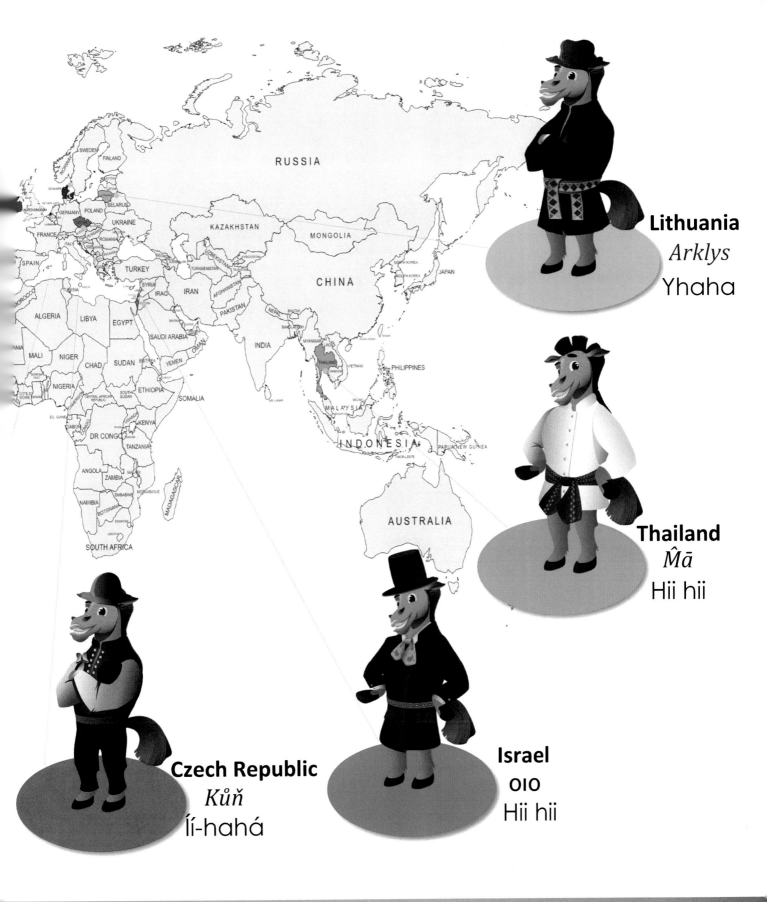

Lithuania
Arklys
Yhaha

Thailand
M̂ā
Hii hii

Czech Republic
Kůň
Íí-hahá

Israel
OIO
Hii hii

🐎 A baby horse is called a foal, or a colt.

🐎 Fun fact: Horses like sweet flavors and will usually reject anything sour or bitter.

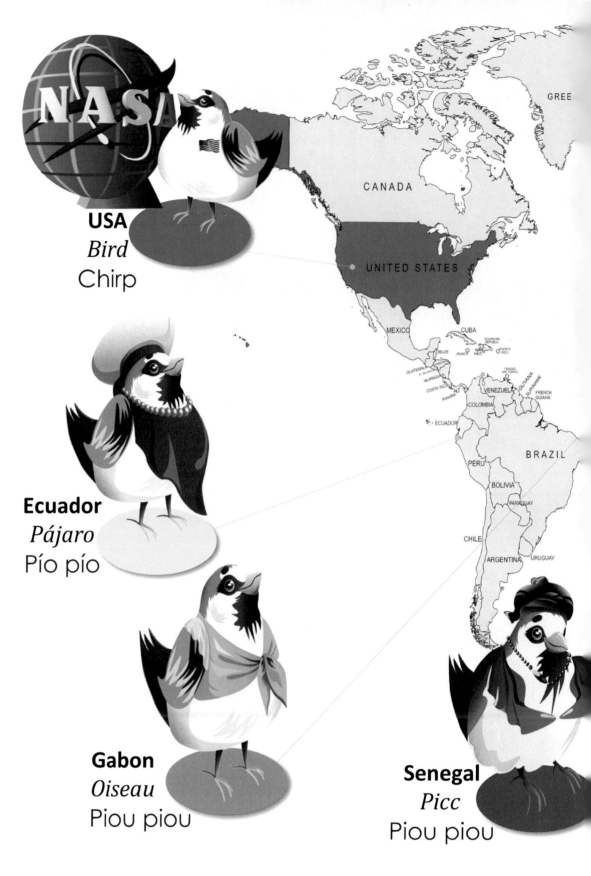

USA
Bird
Chirp

Ecuador
Pájaro
Pío pío

Gabon
Oiseau
Piou piou

Senegal
Picc
Piou piou

A group of birds is called a flock, a volery or a dove.

A male bird is called a cockbird.

A female bird is called a hen.

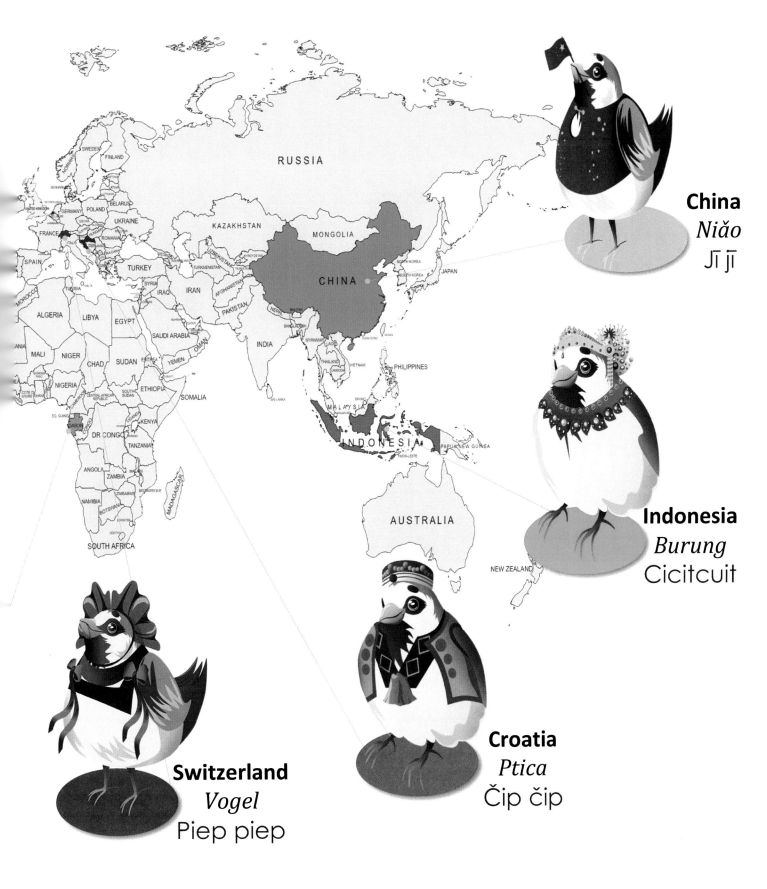

China
Niǎo
Jī Jī

Indonesia
Burung
Cicitcuit

Croatia
Ptica
Čip čip

Switzerland
Vogel
Piep piep

A baby bird is called a hatchling or a chick.

Fun fact: Many scientists believe that birds evolved from dinosaurs about 150 million years ago.

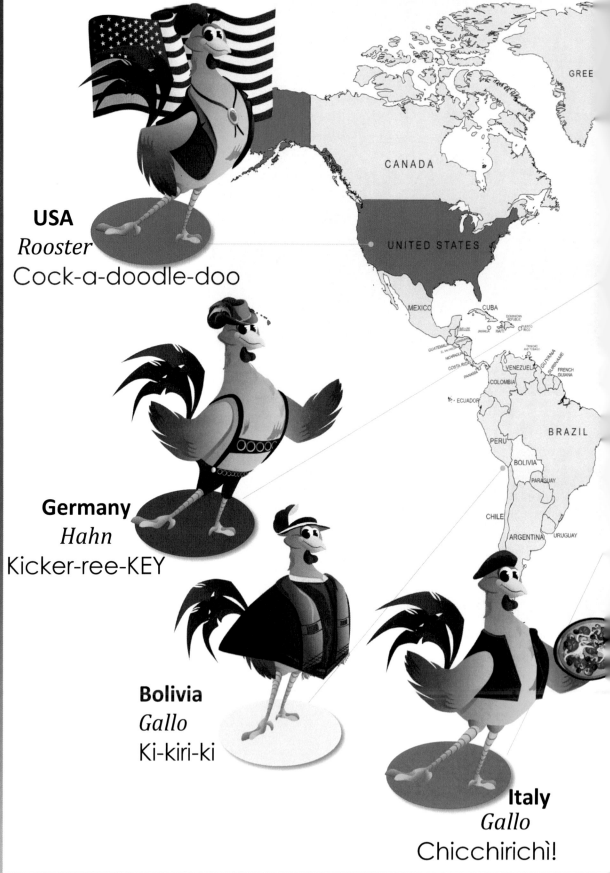

USA
Rooster
Cock-a-doodle-doo

Germany
Hahn
Kicker-ree-KEY

Bolivia
Gallo
Ki-kiri-ki

Italy
Gallo
Chicchirichì!

A group of roosters is called a flock.

A male chicken is called a rooster.

A female chicken is called a hen.

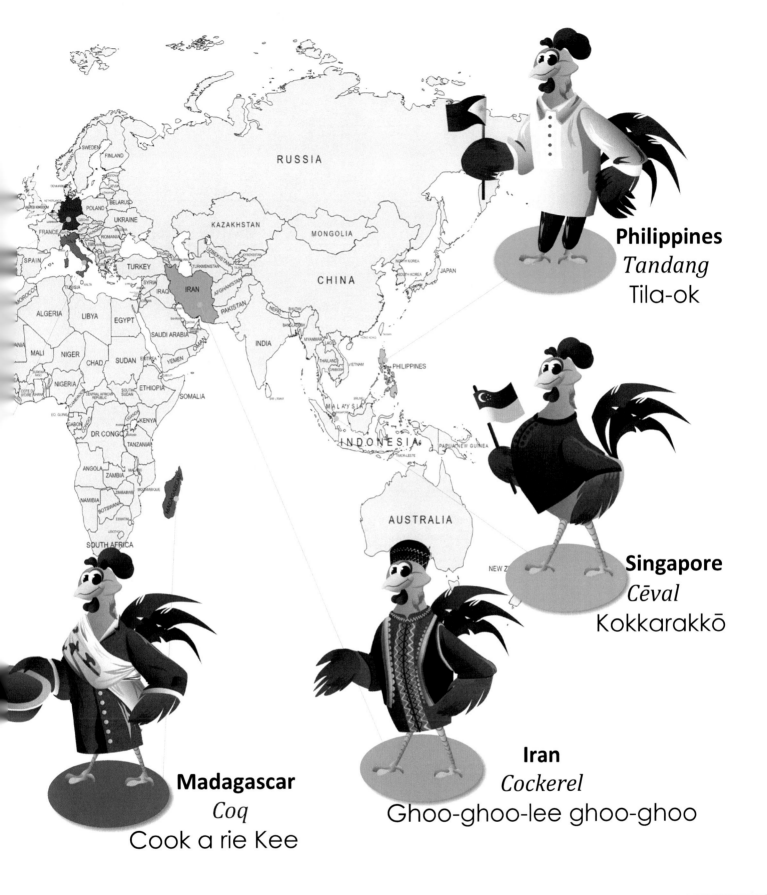

Philippines
Tandang
Tila-ok

Singapore
Cēval
Kokkarakkō

Madagascar
Coq
Cook a rie Kee

Iran
Cockerel
Ghoo-ghoo-lee ghoo-ghoo

🐓 A baby chicken is called a chick.

🐓 Fun fact: Chickens can remember over 100 different faces of people or animals.

USA
Sheep
Baa

Belgium
Mouton
Bêêh

Bolivia
Oveja
Beee

Tunisia
Khuruf
Maa'

A group of sheep is called a flock, a herd, or a drove.

A male sheep is called a ram.

A female sheep is called a ewe.

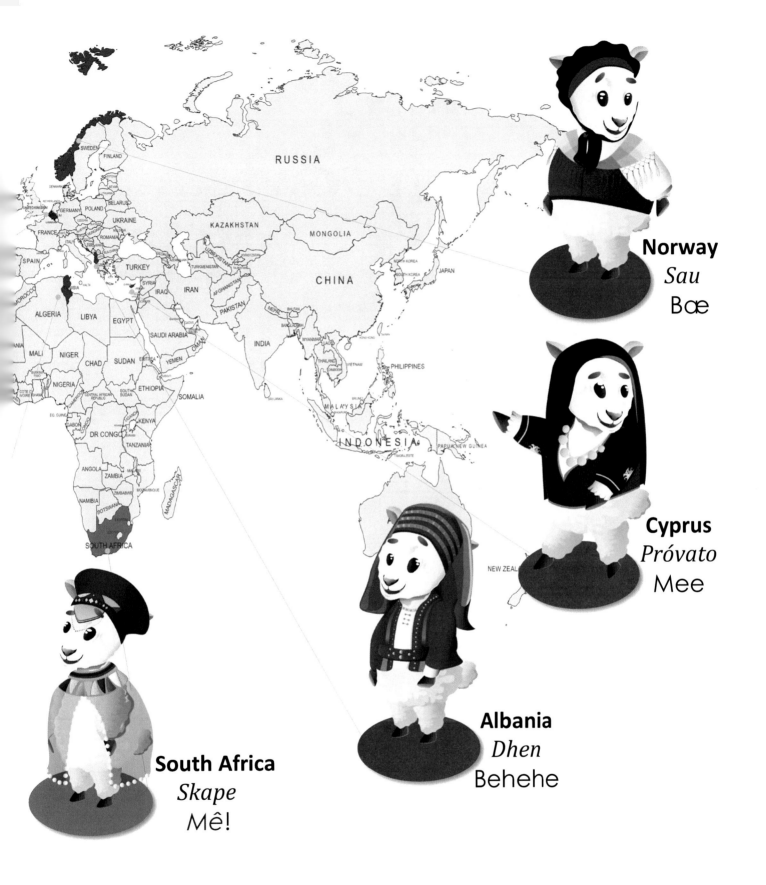

Norway
Sau
Bœ

Cyprus
Próvato
Mee

South Africa
Skape
Mê!

Albania
Dhen
Behehe

🐑 A baby sheep is called a lamb.

🐑 Fun fact: During World War I, President Woodrow Wilson had a flock of sheep trim the White House lawn.

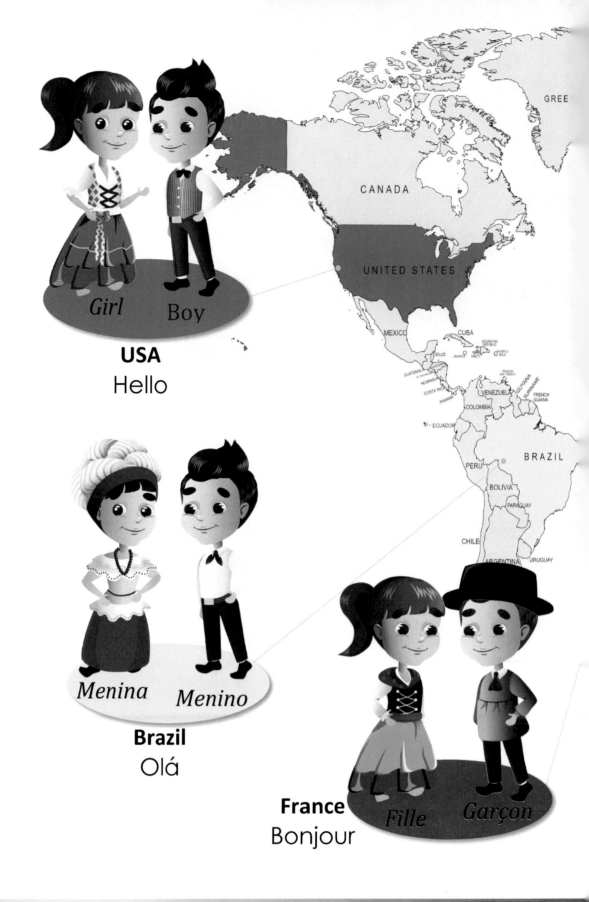

USA
Hello

Brazil
Olá

France
Bonjour

Girl *Boy*

Menina *Menino*

Fille *Garçon*

A group of humans is called a group or a gathering.

A human male is called a boy or a man.

A human female is called a girl or a woman.

Japan
Kon'nichiwa

Otoko no ko   *Onna no ko*

România
Bună

Băiat   *Fată*

Tanzania
Hujambo

Mvulana   *Msichana*

A human baby is called a newborn (ages 0–4 weeks), an infant (ages 4 weeks – 1 year), a toddler (ages 12 months-24 months), a preschooler (ages 2–5 years), a school-aged child (ages 6–12).

Canada
Hello

Guatemala
Hola

UK
Hello

Fun facts: It is impossible to lick your own elbow.

Your nose and ears continue growing for your entire life.

Human teeth are as strong as shark teeth.

Russia
Zdravstvuyt

Devochka *Mal'chik*

Nánhái *Nǔhái*

China
Nǐ hǎo

Niña *Niño*

Spain
Hola

It is impossible to sneeze with your eyes open.

Scientists estimate that the nose can recognize a trillion different scents.

When listening to music, your heartbeat will sync with the rhythm.

Made in the USA
Las Vegas, NV
17 January 2024